John Keyes is an actor and theatre reviewer. He has edited *Robert Harbinson: Selected Stories* (Lagan Press, 1996) and *Sam Thompson: Over the Bridge & Other Plays* (Lagan Press, 1997). A memoir of his early acting career at Belfast's Group and Arts Theatres, *Going Dark: Two Ulster Theatres*, has recently been published recently by Lagan Press.

THE IMPORTANCE OF BEING MICHEÁL

Published by
Lagan Press
138 University Avenue
Belfast BT7 5GZ

ISBN: 1 873687 83 4

Author: John Keyes
Title: The Importance of Being Micheál
2002

Cover: John Keyes as Micheál mac Líammóir
in *The Importance of Being Micheál*
(*photographs by Chris Hill Photography*)
Set in New Baskerville
Printed by Noel Murphy Printing, Belfast

THE IMPORTANCE
OF BEING MICHEÁL

JOHN KEYES

LAGAN PRESS
BELFAST
2002

in memory of my mother
Jeanie Chalmers Keys

THE IMPORTANCE OF BEING MICHEÁL

The Importance of Being Micheál was first performed on 13th February 2002 at Cultúrlann McAdam Ó Fiaich, Belfast. All parts were played by John Keyes. The play was produced by North Face Theatre Company and was directed by Paddy Scully.

ACT I

16th October, 1969. RTE Studios, Dublin. A dressing room. Dressing table, mirror, sofa and armchair. Comfortably furnished. Flowers.

Old man enters. Looks around room. He wears overcoat draped over shoulders and a fedora hat. There is music coming from a tannoy. Tannoy rattles into announcement.

VOICE: Half an hour, please, Mr. mac Líammóir. Can I say, sir, a very happy birthday? What is it, sir? Seventy, is it? Janey mac but you don't look it. Happy birthday to a great Irish man. They're all out there waitin' on you.

MAC LÍAMMÓIR [*to himself*]: Sixty-nine when there are pink lights, seventy when there are not. [*Pause*] They all want one last look before I drop off my perch.

as DUBLIN GOSSIP: We were in the third row from the front because my Dinny has a first cousin who's an assistant to the assistant floor manager. Yes! I saw it with my own two eyes—I swear! And poor Gay trying to put a dignified face on it. And the style! What? Well from where I sat he looked like Mousy Tung playing Baby Jane—honest! In front of the whole world and his mother too!

MAC LÍAMMÓIR: Well, of course Dublin has always thought it *was* the whole world. [*Goes to dresser. Opens box. Takes out large magnifying glass. Picks up list. Lights cigarettes like a blind man. Looks at list. Throws it away in disgust as he is unable to read it.*] What do I need a guest list for? Mary Rose McMaster. Darling Mary Rose. My favourite niece. Michael Redgrave. Dear Michael. Thanks to him and Rachel *Oscar* went to London. Then the world. At least I had that. And Denis Johnston. *The*

Old Lady Says 'No'! changed Irish writing. For about twenty minutes. But when it came to the crunch at the bankrupt Gate poor Denis spent so much time sitting on the fence that I fear the iron entered his soul.

Maybe this old lady should say no.

And Dev. Sweet Eamon who personally signed the passport of this Grand Broth of an Irishman in those early, heady days. The father of the nation. Dancing children and thatched cottages with no running water. No, thank you. All the same ...

And I bet she's there in the front. Siobhán McKenna. Lovely Irish. Picked up in Galway on the way from the Falls Road in Belfast. And mine was picked up—where? ... so long ago. Dangerous woman. 'But I was BORN to play St. Joan!' She nearly stabbed me though the throat in Brussels in the second act—and don't tell me it was an accident!

They'll all be out there—the living and the dead. Eoin? Man of action. New Ireland—1933—forging links with our brothers in Europe—fashion statements in black, brown and blue shirts. Just a little on the common side, I thought. Mind you, an armoured car at the stage door of the Gate to swish one up to Jammets added a certain brio to a penniless existence. Just as well they made him something big in the Gardai.

And Noël sends his love. How very nice. I simply love his little diaries. [*He is tired. He sits at dressing table.*]

The Hollywood Connection. Nothing from Orson. Too preoccupied with his begging bowl somewhere I suppose. Mmm—but a telegram from Helen of Troy. Better known as Eartha Kitt. Such are the quick and the soon to be joined.

Yeats. Of course, if there must be a villain of the piece, then he fits the bill—William Butler Yeats. Oh yes, I blame him entirely for the whole thing. He seduced me, he beguiled me and bewitched me with his magnificent words. But for him, I certainly wouldn't be spending my seventieth birthday in an Irish television studio.

But oh, the missing names! Dearest Mac. Anew McMaster. No, I don't want to think of Mac dead—not tonight.

Now, I'd better get my story straight before I go out there. The beast of sensation must be fed. Give them a dollop of gossip followed by a mouthful of forbidden romance. Titillate their curiosity with the smorgasbord of story and make-believe. In an age of True Confessions and Prodigality, truth and reality would seem surplus and all too mundane.

Sixty years ago. London in late summer. *Please, sir, can I have some more?* I was playing Oliver Twist to Tree's Fagin. Sir Herbert Beerbohm Tree, in case you didn't know.

And there was a special matinée at the command of the King. Every great star in London was there, playing tiny parts. Those two familiar faces in the royal box. [*Inclines head in direction of royal box*]

In the presence of real, rather than stage, royalty Henry V's horse became over excited and committed what you might call a nuisance on the stage. In fact it committed two or three nuisances, one directly on the Queen of France's train. And distinctly soured the temper of Lady Macbeth.

Afterwards, the reception. There, seated on a gilt stage throne, she received us. It was worse than a first night—an audience with Madame Bernhardt. The Divine Sarah. The lace at her wrists and throat, still, eerily still as I bent over to kiss her hand. Gummed. Spirit gummed to her wrists and neck to look beautiful.

Oh God, there's nobody like that now.

as MCMASTER: Except maybe yourself, dear ...

MAC LÍAMMÓIR: Mac would say. Cheek of the devil. But the charm ...

as MCMASTER: So, you got what you wanted, Micky dear—public adoration from Kathleen Ni Houlihan, your adopted bilingual mammie. And for that you have me to thank.

MAC LÍAMMÓIR: Maybe. On the other hand it might have been a KC from Buck House.

as MCMASTER: Never in a million years! Not with your background and that *grand amour fou* with all things Celtic and Gaelic. And how would you explain a knighthood to the ghost of the lovely sad cousin—what was her name?

MAC LÍAMMÓIR: Máire O'Keefe—Máire of the slanted, green, witch's eyes.

We learned Irish at the Sinn Féin centre at Ludgate Hill. And talked of Ireland all day long. And of the great things that would happen there when we all went home.

Home.

Of course, it was all Yeats' fault. Oh yes, I blame him entirely. I had just read his 'Ireland and the Artist'. It changed my life. Entirely.

And then after 1916—all was changed, changed utterly. And a terrible beauty was born. Was it? I wonder. So did he. *Did certain lines of mine ... ?*

And *then* Máire and I and her mother did go back. On seas of emotion and love.

MAC LÍAMMÓIR: I'll join the IRA.

as MÁIRE: You!

MAC LÍAMMÓIR: Máire thought this was hilarious. [*Pause*] Well, of course, it was.

as MÁIRE: Micky, darling, if you really want to see Ireland free, please, please keep away from the fighting.

MAC LÍAMMÓIR: So Máire, Craven, her mother, and I lived in a tiny cottage on Howth. I went into the city daily, avoiding the Black and Tans who looked at us with some suspicion. Twice they raided the cottage and took away Sinn Féin literature. But they were puzzled. Craven and Máire's accents were distinctly middle-class English; and Craven's sister, on a November visit, had insisted on selling poppies in Howth village and had worn a coat bedecked with Union Jacks.

And I had met George Russell. Æ. Had gone to tea with him and he had bought a few of my pictures. And talked of Ireland. And of magic. And Yeats, whom he promised to introduce me to.

It didn't happen. I had to wait for years to meet the man who gave my life whatever shape it has.

But he introduced me to the Abbey Theatre where I made friends who would last the rest of my life. Arthur Shields and his brother, Barry Fitzgerald. Maureen Delaney, who took me under her capacious wing. And I played a small part in an early production. Can't remember what.

But the Abbey was not for me. Its certainties, far too certain. And its heights—apart from its bright stars, McCormack, Delaney and Algood—were not high.

And then, again, was it acting? Was it theatre? Talking about the English actor manager, George Alexander, who had first produced his plays, Oscar Wilde had said, churlishly, that: 'He doesn't act; he behaves.'

I always thought that this could have been said of the Abbey. But its behaviour was Irish, not English. And apart from Yeats, whose plays could be guaranteed to empty the house, we had found no new form—we had nothing new to say. And the Abbey didn't understand Yeats at all. And couldn't do his plays.

I dreamed of finding a new Irish voice. A voice that was Irish and European rather than provincial English and a voice that was not defined by accent, Dublin or the mist that does be on the bog. But was clearly, indisputably itself.

And it wasn't until years later when Denis Johnston wrote *The Old Lady Says 'No'!* and Hilton and I produced it at the Gate, that I heard it. That the great bell tolled.

Who were we then? Who, indeed?

as MCMASTER: Just another mad bunch of romantic English half-wits looking for a lost cause maybe?

MAC LÍAMMÓIR: Shut up, Mac—you'll soon enough get your solo spot.

But we were on the move again for Máire was carrying a burden that was not uncommon then—another victim of the scourge of Tuberculosis—and for the next few years we scraped a living visiting the spas and sanitoriums across Europe. My training at the Slade came in useful and I made some money selling my pictures. Talked. Learned languages. I was fluent, though inaccurate, in many. But it was a tiring battle for Máire that came to an end in Monte Carlo.

And suddenly she was dead. *Old Death's bony finger will never find us here.* We quoted Yeats to each other. In London fogs. On the tube. On the Hill of Howth. In Europe. But it was there in Monte Carlo that it found her.

She went on talking right up to the end. Couldn't die. Talked right up to the last. From her beautiful tired face I could tell that she could hear the death rattle in her own throat.

After the funeral her mother and I put on our gayest clothes and went to the Ballets Russes. It was *Le Train Bleu*. With Diaghilev's newest prodigy; Anton Dolin—Paddy Healey Kay from Co. Wicklow.

It was years before I knew he was Irish. Of course, you had to change your name then if you wanted to to be taken seriously as a dancer. It was a fact universally acknowledged that if you were English or Irish you couldn't put one foot in front of another.

In the interval we met Noël Coward and Ivor Novello. Back to the beginning: Noël and I in *The Goldfish*. Me in *Peter Pan*. Noël in *Where the Rainbow Ends*. And Ivor, already a great star. We both envied him then. And wondered about ourselves. They asked us why we were crying. We hadn't realised that we were.

Who could have seen us all together thirty-five years later at the Coliseum? *Where the Rainbow Ends*. Pat as St. George. 'What England has she holds.' It wasn't long after Suez. And me as the Wicked Dragon King—Irish, of course—all set to destroy England's Majesty. And failing. What chance had an Irish Dragon against St. George of England?

I introduced Noël to Máire's mother and he asked if I'd told her how we met.

My first audition for Lila Field and *The Goldfish*. In Act I, I played Prince Mussell and sang vivaciously. In Act II we all changed into fairies.

Some of us have remained fairies to this day.

as LILA: Now, children. What do you think of my stage? Here's the garden seat. And *there's* the magic pool. No, Philip, not there, *there*. That's right, dear, do try and concentrate. Prince Mussell, dear, you're not on for half an hour. Go and talk to Prince Hal. Master Noël, entertain Master Michael.

MAC LÍAMMÓIR: It was like Stanley meeting Livingstone in the wilds of Holland Park.

as YOUNG MAC LÍAMMÓIR: Hello.

as YOUNG NOËL COWARD: How do you do?

as YOUNG MAC LÍAMMÓIR: Ah, how do you do?

as YOUNG NOËL COWARD: Lozenge?

as YOUNG MAC LÍAMMÓIR: Thanks.

as YOUNG NOËL COWARD: They're supposed to encourage conversation. Personally, I have never found them of the smallest use. But then I have never had any difficulty with conversation. Still, you look as though you could do with one.

as YOUNG MAC LÍAMMÓIR: Thanks. What do you think of the show?

as YOUNG NOËL COWARD: Very silly indeed. And very badly written. But it's an engagement. The Scala will be alright, and the Hackney Empire, but then we play Manchester. Have you played Manchester?

as YOUNG MAC LÍAMMÓIR: No.

as YOUNG NOËL COWARD: You were quite right. It's dreadful. Perfectly dreadful. Gertie Lawrence and I had bed bugs in Ackers Street.

as YOUNG MAC LÍAMMÓIR: What are you going to be when you grow up?

as YOUNG NOËL COWARD: Why, an actor, of course. There's nothing else but the theatre, you know. You?

as YOUNG MAC LÍAMMÓIR: I ... I'm not sure.

as YOUNG NOËL COWARD: You should always be quite sure what you want to do. Otherwise you will waste time.

as YOUNG MAC LÍAMMÓIR: We're only *eleven.*

as YOUNG NOËL COWARD: Quite. There's so much to do. Now, do forgive me. I'm writing a little song for myself in Act II. I think Miss Field will like it.

as YOUNG MAC LÍAMMÓIR: Is she good?

as YOUNG NOËL COWARD: Don't be ridiculous, dear boy.

MAC LÍAMMÓIR: I wish I had taken Noël's advice. I have always known where I wanted to be and with whom. But what? Ah no.

Europe had for the moment lost its charms for us. And Craven returned to London.

After Máire's death in 1927, the European years ended. For years I had been in a kind of dream. Painfully, I began to awake.

When someone you love dies, life seems like a waiting room, dusty and interminable. It is like this for a long time.

And I began to long for Ireland. And Mac. And the longings were for the past.

Me, at eleven, playing Oliver Twist; Mac, eighteen, in *The Scarlet Pimpernel*, at the New. The stage doors were opposite each other in an alley leading from Tottenham Court Road to St. Martin's Lane.

Mac was a Greek God. I, Ganymede. And my sister, Marjorie, who looked after me. And listened. Always listened. As Mac and I talked of Ireland. And other things. And he was only interested in the theatre. And I was interested in him.

When he went to Ireland in 1914, Marjorie was livid. 'England needs every man she can get.' And she knitted for the troops. She read *The Times*, frantically. Worried. And knitted some more. But she never stopped loving him—that would have been impossible no matter what he said of you.

as MCMASTER: Puccini, dear, that's you on the stage. All wine and roses, Mediterranean air and moonlight. You're not Wagnerian. I don't suppose you want to be. Not that I'm saying ... Oh no, dear. You're very good, *very* good and God knows I love Puccini. But great acting is Fire and Wind, you see.

MAC LÍAMMÓIR: Oh yes. But why have *you* stopped?

as MCMASTER: Flash in the pan, dear. That's me in Dublin. Anyway it's too small. Everybody thinks they can do everything. No discipline. Plenty of genius, of course. Not enough talent.

They've got to love you when you act. I found that out myself at Stratford this year. At Stratford they will. In London they will. In Dublin they will for a week or two—then they'll turn on you. I told you Micheál, it's too small to live in.

And you're worse than me. Oh yes, you see with me it was strictly personal, dear. Personal. All I need is a stage. Ireland gives me that.

But with you? Oh no. There's this national thing. Romantic Republicanism. Oh Micky, I can't tell you how dangerous it is for an artist to get mixed up in that. It's a waste of time.

You and your Yeats. And Ireland. And a language that only half a dozen people speak. I'm a gypsy, dear. I can be happy anywhere I can play my parts. But not you. No, Micheál. A great mistake.

as DUBLINER: 'Ah, you were fierce, Mr. Mac, you were fierce.'
MAC LÍAMMÓIR: So he was. Fierce.

'Anew McMaster & His World Famous Company'.

Othello. In the middle of nowhere.

And they came streaming down the mountains in their horses and carts eager for the thrill. Still reeling from a vicious civil war. But they came in for Shakespeare, of all things.

Oh yes. *He* was fire and wind and passion. Such passion in all those tiny grey Irish towns. How they loved him. Too big for them? Ah, not at all. Because, you see, the Irish love sound, love words, love Shakespeare. No visual sense at all, of course. Look at the Abbey 'til they got Tanya Moiseiwitsch. 'Til Hilton and I showed them design. Some of them would still have preferred an old couch and a po under the bed.

Not exactly His Majesty's Theatre and the Haymarket. And King George and Queen Mary and Tree. But, my God, it was theatre!

Mac and his theatre took my mind off Máire's death. Life is like that. You're sitting in that dreary waiting room. Then suddenly, lifting your head, you see a poster that attracts your attention.

And, as though you had dreamed it all, you're in a train whistling away God knows where. Smoking, talking, sharing your food with other passengers, and gazing out of the windows.

But the waiting room is in your soul, and you never quite get rid of it. Oh no.

You hardly, indeed, want to.

It was time to go back. To Ireland, of course. But to the theatre where all things are possible. And I went back to Mac.

At this time in 1928, Anew McMaster, now by some bizarre and ironic twist of fate, my brother-in-law, which I privately thought had been adding incest to injury, had been running his own Shakespearean company touring all over Ireland.

I met him in London where he was rehearsing for a short tour of the more genteel English towns before going back home. And eight weeks later, the company met at Euston Station to get the night boat to Dun Laoghaire. Waiting and waiting.

But Mac carried drama around with him like a cloak when he finally appeared with Marjorie.

as MCMASTER: Oh yes, my dears. We've been 'Let Down' again! Of course, I never expect anything else. Never. It was just the same with Sarah. Now Marjorie and I have to stay here and find an Iago, a new King in *Hamlet*, a Macduff, not to mention a Professor Van Helsing in *Dracula*. And a few other things as well. So you *won't* open in Enniscorthy on Monday—and God knows when you will. Oh well, I told poor old David that we'd keep a candle in the window for him. When he's better. But a fat lot of good that does us now.

Anyway, expect us in Ireland when you see us.

MAC LÍAMMÓIR: And all night over the swelling sea I dreamed that I was waking up after a long convalescence; that the dim twilight was breaking into little blots and blobs of brightness. And that day was knocking insistently on my eyelids.

In Enniscorthy we waited for Mac and Marjorie to come back with whatever they could find at such short notice. Coralie Carmichael, Mac's leading lady, and I found that we were friends, the friends of a lifetime. And we rehearsed what we could. And we ate rashers and eggs, walked in the sun, and slept in bedrooms which were positive shambles of holy pictures. And, a couple of days later, at the rather grandly named Athenaeum, May Barry, the wardrobe mistress, told us:

_as_ MAY BARRY: Four years at the Old Vic; and he's a singer too. Now, I wouldn't say, mind you, that he was terrible tall—he's kind of medium. He has a big nose and he's what you would say, decided. Oh, he's real manly, but a nice polished way of speaking—though he's English, of course, God help him. Ah, he's falling to bits with the journey. Mr. Mac says he's paying him a desperate salary. Well, sure you couldn't expect him to come on summer terms. Ah, thanks be to God Mr. Mac has him rooted out.

MAC LÍAMMÓIR: Naturally, we formed a composite picture of Schnozzle Durante, an all-in wrestler, a diplomatist, an uncompromising John Bull, an historical ruin and a bloated capitalist. We were alarmed.

I wandered out of the theatre and waited in the sun. It was the Feast of Corpus Christi.

Immediately, I heard Mac's voice in the pitch he quite genuinely believed to be his only audible one:

_as_ MCMASTER [_to_ HILTON]: Yes, my brother-in-law. Designs the scenery for us as well. Quite mad, but very charming. [_To_ MAC LÍAMMÓIR] Ah, there you are, Micheál, how are you? [_Referring to_ HILTON] _Much_ the best I could find, dear. _Marvellous_ audition, _bloody_ expensive, can't be helped. Mana's exhausted, digs too _terrible_, dear. Bitch of a landlady. [_To_ HILTON]Here we are, Hilton. This is my brother-in-law, Micheál mac Líammóir. This is our new Iago, Micheál, Mr. Hilton Edwards.

_as_ HILTON: How do you do?

MAC LÍAMMÓIR: How do you do?

Our friendship established itself rapidly in spite of or perhaps _because_ of our seemingly endless differences. His energy was apparently without end. So was his patience. Especially in stage matters. And, in action, his clarity and concentration were astonishing.

All that summer we worked. Up to ten different shows a week. Mostly Shakespeare, with *Dracula* or *Fu Manchu* on Sunday nights. For light relief. Not that we needed them. For the audiences wanted Shakespeare. But Mac loved playing the fiendish, oriental Fu Manchu. And Coralie nightly saved her virtue from him by a hair's breadth for several months.

I had written my first play in Irish, *Diarmuid agus Gráinne* and Mac had agreed to do an English translation on tour. It was billed for Kilkenny. 'Anew McMaster in *Diarmuid and Gráinne* by Micheál mac Líammóir.'

But the weeks passed and there was no sign of rehearsal. And at last he said:

as MCMASTER: It's not the time for it, dear. We're all exhausted and we've just done *The Dream*. No, I can't face it—just can't face it. Even the Divine Sarah couldn't face new plays all the time, Micheál. We'll do it in the spring.

MAC LÍAMMÓIR: And I knew that there was no argument.

And later in the pub with Coralie, Hilton said. 'We'll do it. We'll build a theatre in Dublin even if it's just to do your bloody play.'

And there it was.

Well, actually, there it wasn't. Neither of us had a bean.

But when he gets an idea, Hilton is like an elephant trampling down obstacles, moving towards his goal. Not like me at all.

I could have happily discussed the new theatre for months on end, if not years. The productions we would do. The new techniques we would use. And all without moving out of the snug. Where so many Irish works of genius have been conceived—and stillborn.

In the meantime there was another Mac tour. We saved every penny that we could for the new theatre in Dublin. Hilton arranged an exhibition of my pictures in Cork, and really, they sold astonishingly well. I arranged singing dates for him in Dublin and Derry. And he recorded some songs for the BBC in London.

And things began to happen.

One morning when the Mac company was playing in Galway, the landlady told me that Professor Líam O Bríain of Galway University wanted to see me.

And, for the first time, I saw the small laughing eyes. And heard the cackling, irresistible laughter of my best Galway friend.

We spoke in Irish and I wondered if it were a dream. For here was the offer of a real theatre and a chance to produce *Diarmuid agus Gráinne* in its own language.

And to produce it on a stage in the only Irish-speaking town we had left could make a model that might have results for the future.

The future.

We Irish are accused of eternally brooding over the images of the past. But in reality it is by the future, more it may be than any other people in the world, that we are driven.

For the vision of a most questionable posterity that we walk out of our homes, that we dream and plot and play the fool and suffer and die.

We have created a past for ourselves that we may more clearly see the future of our heart's desire. And in the continual striving and sacrifice offered up for that future lies, perhaps, the only Irish virtue.

Listening to Líam gave me a glimpse of a possible future.

Would I be producer? Would I also consider opening the theatre with my own play ?

Would I train a group of amateurs from Connemara and Aran, who had never seen a play in their lives, to be actors?

Would I come to Galway to live?

My enthusiasm rose and fell.

At that time, Galway had a desolate and undeniable beauty and fascination. My love for the language was real enough, God knows, and the experience would be invaluable.

But after my first, gushing reception of the project—I am one who gushes easily and with a complete, if only momentary, sincerity—I began to wonder how much I welcomed the idea.

For an actor to work in Ireland at all demands a certain denial. A certain holding back from the important Grand Finals of the race.

But to bury oneself deliberately in a language spoken only by a few thousand souls, most of whom are oblivious to any sense of the theatre? Was not this lunacy?

But the temptation was strong. I told Hilton.

To my total astonishment, he approved. But Líam wanted me to start immediately.

as LÍAM O BRÍAIN: You'll have to supervise the building of the stage; and the lights. Is docha go dtuigeann tu na rudai seo go lier?

MAC LÍAMMÓIR: But no, I didn't understand these things at all. And Líam said:

as LÍAM O BRÍAIN: Well, will the two of you come? For God's sake, this has to happen. It's going to be marvellous. The first Irish speaking theatre in the world. Now! In the name of God, will you both come?

MAC LÍAMMÓIR: We said we would think it over.

And we left it like that.

The final curtain came down on my last Mac tour in June. And I left them with regret. For Mac and Marjorie were institutions in my life and I could not imagine things without them somewhere.

Besides, Mac had taught me so much about art, about life.

So, while I lived in Galway with Mrs. Katie Ward in her pub, trudged daily over the town with Líam O Bríain looking for premises, talked to anyone who might turn out to be an actor and started work on rehearsals of *Diarmuid agus Gráinne*, Hilton went to London to get advice on forming an experimental arts theatre.

When he came back he was full of it all.

But I had doubts. Was all this just a touch exotic for Dublin?

In London there was a full theatrical banquet for all who wanted to sup. No such feast existed in Ireland where famine in the arts had not encouraged a taste for foreign dishes.

What Dublin had was well cooked cabbage and bacon at the Abbey, stewed prunes and custard at the Gaiety and kickshaws at the music halls and the pictures.

The fact that we had new methods of presentation in mind and that, unlike other organisations, we intended to work with fully professional actors, would not, I thought, cut much ice in Ireland. For Ireland cares a great deal for matter and hardly at all for manner. At least, it did then.

And, though it took me many years fully to realise this, I dimly sensed it even before we had begun our work.

Start as one means to go on, we thought.

The Dublin season would start with *Peer Gynt*, no less. To be followed, in case anyone doubted our seriousness, with O'Neill's *Hairy Ape*, Wilde's *Salome* and the English version of *Diarmuid agus Gráinne*.

My friend Jack Dunne told us: 'Get it on early in the season. These Dublin ventures never last very long.'

But Hilton was sure of himself and his project and was determined that we should last for more than one season.

And back in Galway, I knew we must make an impression and *Diarmuid agus Gráinne* a riot of colour. I had determined on a Bakst-like largesse of colour in the costumes. Gráinne in gold, Diarmuid in copper and peacock blue, Fionn in bronze and green and white and the High King in flame colour and black, and so on. Madame Toto Bannard Cogley, who ran a cabaret in Dublin and had been fired by Hilton's enthusiasm for the Gate—thank God—was making the costumes to my design.

And now we were thrown into the near hysteria that means production. The committee was meeting almost daily, and the mingled excitement of aesthetics and patriotism was going to our heads. Hilton was drawn into this passionate revivalism, and, when on his appearance at the meetings we dropped into English for his benefit, would beg us to go on in Irish and assure us that he was beginning to pick it up.

But his advice was far too valuable to take the risk.

And we went on looking for actors in a city where none existed. Sometimes we despaired.

Apart from directing the play, I was playing Diarmuid myself.

Sometimes, Hilton and I would argue for an hour or more about the precise position of an actor during a speech, and, to our surprise, this drew forth delighted cries from members of the committee.

Da' mbeadh daoine ag ple le mionrudai mar seo fiche blian o shin bhi an Ghaelige sabhailte—If people had paid this much attention to detail twenty years ago, the language would be saved.

And, inexorably, the first night came. And went.

The Dublin papers the next day were enthusiastic and hinted that the west was indeed awake. Which was agreeable to hear, if not strictly true.

Though it was, perhaps, turning over in its bed.

I had never dreamed of Máire. But I knew she was there. How she would have loved it.

And before we knew it, it was time to open in Dublin.

We had taken the Peacock Theatre for the season and the porch was decorated with our new wooden sign with the words 'Dublin Gate Theatre Studio' in letters of gold.

One hundred and one persons would see us for the theatre held one hundred and two and I had bagged the last seat and didn't count as the audience at all.

I have had experience of many first nights in many cities. But that performance of *Peer Gynt* remains, for all time, the most poignant and profound.

We had done it. We had opened our own theatre in Dublin against all odds.

The Dublin press restrained its enthusiasm.

One paper said that Ibsen's verse was wooden, and the choice of play 'unfortunate'. Another, that he was reminded of a penny gaffe. Another that it was a 'praiseworthy effort'. And yet another that Hilton gave a 'good display of activity', a phrase that might have meant anything—and probably did.

But the *Irish Statesman* was full of enthusiasm and the monthlies were encouraging.

The audiences were small but we struggled on.

Of course, there was no question of making any money. Once a floodlamp was smashed at rehearsal. It had cost thirty shillings. And Hilton said: 'There go our profits for a fortnight.'

Diarmuid agus Gráinne was our third play. But the excitement had gone and I felt increasingly unhappy in the world of the Celtic Twilight. These were no times for echoing the vanished rhapsodies of the 90s, and, despite much praise, I began to dislike intensely what I had written.

But the play made me a new and exciting friend. One day a letter arrived from Lady Gregory who had, unknown to me, been to the theatre the previous night. This was important indeed. With Yeats, she had created what was the National Theatre of Ireland.

In those early days we travelled almost always by taxi for the simple reason that we had rarely enough money for buses.

Which seems odd until you remember the trustfulness of Dublin taxi drivers. They all expected to be paid when we started to do well. And they were.

But money was desperately short and Hilton and I living in service flats in Pembroke Street relied on the kindness of Monty and Tessie Martin, our landlords. We began to run up bills.

They came to the shows and gave us drinks and sandwiches afterwards. And all the gossip of the town. Politics, of course. To the Irish the politics of peace are more difficult than those of war.

as **TESSIE MARTIN:** Did you hear? Cosgrave's party is going out soon and de Valéra's coming in. Glad? I'm not. Things'll be just as lousy as they are now, and they'll let all those IRA boys out of jail, and then we'll all be murdered in our beds. In our *beds*! Where will it all end?

Speaking of which, Maud Gonne is going to see your show tonight. Maud Gonne Mad they used to call her. Lovely woman, though. All the men are mad about her.

Yeats is going to live in Rathfarnam. Oh yes, well you can't blame him. Fed up with all those old cats playing bridge all day long in Merrion Square.

Oh, and Mac's bringing over Mrs. Patrick Campbell for Lady Macbeth.

MAC LÍAMMÓIR: Yeats saw us for the first time in *The Unknown Warrior* and I knew it was because he was there that I gave the only performance that came within miles of what I had intended.

I could see him clearly as he sat there with Lady Gregory and I knew that his attention was held.

The next day an invitation came from Lady Gregory to lunch with her and meet the poet. I was a little late—from a prolonged rehearsal. He rose to his feet, tall and slow and stately, as grey as time. As vague and vivid as a dream.

as **YEATS:** You told Lady Gregory you had wanted to meet me for fourteen years. You are exactly fourteen minutes late.

MAC LÍAMMÓIR: I said that it had seemed like forty, and I naturally expected that he would say 'Years or minutes?', to which, like Lady Bracknell, I would have replied, 'Both if necessary, I presume'.

But he wouldn't play.

as **YEATS:** You are a magnificent actor.

MAC LÍAMMÓIR: For this I was genuinely and totally unprepared. I felt on the verge of tears, but there was nothing to do but simper. It was very bad.

The next move was equally unexpected.

as **YEATS:** How do you do?

MAC LÍAMMÓIR: And I was helped to my feet again so that the comedy could recommence.

And, though I knew that it was incorrect to answer this strangely inquisitive, English salutation, I said that I was very well, thank you, and how was he? And was reassured about his health.

So we sat down to lunch and he was meek and obeyed Lady Gregory in choosing roast mutton over curry as the lesser of two evils.

Those who dismiss him as a man by saying that, outside his work, he was an arrogant poseur, cannot have known him.

Of course, he could pose. Of course, he could be rude and arrogant.

He could, indeed, be anything he chose. The ability to wear a mask, to be all those things is a bare necessity of life to anyone who chooses to live his life in Ireland, whose passionate, almost quixotic worship of mediocrity is coupled with an instinctive distrust of the first rate.

What have I earned for all that work, I said.
The daily spite of this unmannerly town.

He asked me for stories of Tree and legends of ghosts in Galway.

And when I got up to go he invited me to his house, and his manner as he stood by Lady Gregory's side, was simple and friendly.

During the second Gate season at the Peacock we found premises. One morning, Michael Scott, the architect, arrived at the flat, plucked us, silently, from beds and baths and, without a word, bundled us into a motor car.

We had inspected everywhere. Moving gradually from central

Dublin to the remotest suburbs. No obscure Dublin highway was a stranger to us. But there was nothing.

'You've found somewhere,' I said to a stony profile. Which remained stony. 'If he has, it'll be on Rathlin Island,' said Hilton. We were driving north. We crossed the Liffey in O'Connell Street. North side, I thought drearily. And on we went. Past Nelson's Column. Past the Post Office and through Parnell Square. And stopped. In front of a lovely, low eighteenth century building in grey stone. The Rotunda. A hospital for Dublin's poor.

At the side of the building was a small pillared entrance up some steps. And we went in. Upstairs, deep in dust and festooned with spiders webs was a large and lovely room, it could have been a ballroom.

Not that I saw its loveliness at all. And Hilton kept leaping about. Most unrestful. What did I think? I didn't know—it was so dark and dirty. But he was in no mood for fastidiousness. What the hell did I expect? Buckingham Palace? And after what seemed many frozen hours we left the building.

Hilton was bubbling.

As we got into the car, he pointed up. There—we'll have the name there. It'll show all the way down O'Connell Street. In electric lights. Just the one word.

Gate.

The Gate. It was done.

We needed a Board to raise money, for the new building would have to be completely redesigned. Handel had once played there. Now we would.

Our distinguished, indeed aristocratic Board, went about its business, raising money.

Hilton designed all the practical necessities for the stage and then Michael Scott took over. We had to ignore the exquisite Georgian ceiling for a reconstruction would have been financially out of the question.

But I painted the walls in dull gold with woodwork in black and scarlet.

The curtain, too, was black with an enormous gate in gold rising out of golden waves.

And we opened with Goethe's *Faust.*

And, while the Abbey company was in America, Mac was playing Macbeth in their theatre to Mrs. Patrick Campbell's Lady M.

It was a tempestuous season.

He came to tea on the first day of rehearsals.

as MCMASTER: Divine, my dears. She's divine, and she's had all her luggage painted green. She wants to stay here, forever. She says she felt Yeats' great spirit all over the theatre. We were rehearsing in the Royal, dear, but she thought it was the Abbey. All that stuff about her being difficult is nonsense. You know it is, Micheál. Jealousy, dear. Just jealousy.

MAC LÍAMMÓIR: But, as the days went on he became a little worn.

as MCMASTER: Of course, she's such a great *actress*, you see. You have to forgive a great actress if she ... well, you just have to overlook these little moments.

I suppose she *is* as great as ... yes, she is. She is! But oh, there are things in her character that—no, I won't say it.

But I wonder if a person who was a great artist could *stoop*— oh, the things she said today. The sulks. The venoms.

Today, dear, I *saw*. Saw with my own eyes what people mean about her. Don't mention her to me. Don't *breathe* her bloody name!

She's a *fiend*, dear, in what may once have been a human shape. Oh well, never again. That's all I can say. Never again.

Well, there you are. It's no use. And I shall always adore the wicked bitch. You see, in spite of everything, she's such an incredible *artist.*

MAC LÍAMMÓIR: And we opened with *Faust.* It was winter. And the heating failed. The play is long. But the applause was tumultuous and the enthusiasm, as Queen Victoria would have said, most gratifying. And the party onstage afterwards, in spite of red noses and fur coats was, like the play, a huge success.

How strange that a play in which a man sells his soul to the devil should be so popular in Holy Ireland.

Coralie and Hilton and I raised our glasses and remembered the pub in Galway.

We had done it. And we would again and again.

Three years later we were on the verge of bankruptcy. We were in need of a miracle.

Soon, the Dear Old Gate would be only a beautiful memory and Hilton and I would be climbing the agents' stairs in London, hoping for a double engagement in pantomime.

I listened. It isn't true that I spend time at committee meetings drawing Chinese faces on the agenda. But speeches are so dull, while the speakers' faces are so interesting, begging to be drawn.

Besides. I didn't believe in all those Cassandra voices. For my own voices, as clear as those of Jeanne d'Arc, told me with ringing clarity that the Gate wasn't finished at all. There were 700 shares left unsold. So it was no surprise to me at all when a stout young man with rosy cheeks and an Etonian accent rose to his feet and said:

as LORD LONGFORD: I-I-I wish to purchase the remaining shares and my cheque is ready whenever it is needed.

MAC LÍAMMÓIR: And there was pandemonium. Who was it? And I was told. That's Lord Longford. And the Longford regime began.

But we were learning all the time.

And learning costs money.

Without Edward and Christine Longford there is no doubt that the Gate would have gone under. But with Edward it changed, radically.

Edward was in love with the theatre. More specifically, he was in love with the Gate. It was a wonderful clockwork toy. And he wanted to know how it worked.

More dangerously for Hilton and me, he wanted to work it himself.

But there were no dark thoughts of serpents being nourished in bosoms. In the early days the skies were blue with no sepulchral storm warnings at all.

And they were *fun*. Edward was a passionate nationalist and his strongly held political opinions—much stronger than mine—rang out in accents usually only to be heard on the playing fields of Eton.

At the Dublin Horse Show, he had once pulled a man's hat down over his ears for standing for 'God Save the King'.

And he wrote one or two very good plays indeed. *The Yahoos* gave Hilton, as Swift, one of his finest parts.

Then the rows began. Edward tried to influence casting while Hilton and I, reared in traditions as inflexible as the Samurai, believed that casting was the business of the director.

Despite his nationalism, it was Edward's idea that we should play in London.

Naturally, Hilton and I were delighted but careful.

For the English speaking actor, London is Mecca. This may be regrettable but it is, nonetheless, a fact.

We were to take three plays: *The Old Lady Says 'No'!*, *The Yahoos*, and, to the great disapproval of Hilton and me, *Hamlet.*

Hamlet.

To London.

Not unlike the Irish Coal Board advertising its product in Newcastle on Tyne.

The wonder was that John Gielgud didn't think to send *The Playboy* to Dublin with himself as Christy Mahon.

But then again, Edward was so kind.

as **LORD LONGFORD:** Now, let's see. How are we doing with this one? Yes, not very good, is it. Very well, I'll give you a cheque.

MAC LÍAMMÓIR: And he wrote one out and gave it to our secretary, Isa Hughes, who put it away saying, piously, 'The Lord Will Provide.' She was a wicked Protestant. We forgot that if the Lord could provide, the Lord could take away.

And so we flocked into London like a plague of Irish locusts on a summer outing.

And for the first two plays the critics and public were delighted. And talked of Irish Passion, and Irish Imagination and Irish Everything Else.

But for *Hamlet* they were definitely muted. One even referred to me as a 'broth' of a Hamlet.

Serves me right.

But there were pleasant moments. A party of old gentlemen rushed round after one performance to tell me I was the

Hamlet they had waited for for years. Showing, surely, a remarkable patience on their part.

And at another performance, as I had said, 'This is I, Hamlet, the Dane,' a voice from the circle shouted, 'Good Boy. Exactly where Irving paused.'

So London was both a success and a failure. And I felt as though I were in a dream.

I wandered around the streets of the city which once had been mine, and saw ghosts at every corner.

The lights still blazed in Shaftesbury Avenue. And there was John Gielgud in *Richard of Bordeaux*. And the names that blazed most beautifully were Laurence Olivier, Ivor Novello, Michael Redgrave, Peggy Ashcroft, Edith Evans and Noël Coward.

Oh well, I thought, they would soon forget. And then we would come back.

I didn't visit the suburb where I had spent my childhood. I was afraid.

So, in the meantime, we went home, to Dublin.

I had translated Shaw's *Arms and the Man* into Irish and after the production in Galway, my work in the west was finished.

And in Dublin, I was offered the producership of *An Comhar Drammíochta*, the Gaelic Drama League of Dublin. There was a new production every four weeks. And our own theatre was rented for two playing nights every month. Rehearsals took place between six and seven in a bare room in Parnell Square. In addition to our own productions, I had been doing this for five years.

In all activities associated with the revival of the Irish language there is the oddest mix of talent, exuberance intrigue, jealousy, idleness, avarice and devotion. Coupled with high spirits and a lack of any sense of time.

Especially British Mean Time.

I fretted at every rehearsal. But if any comment were made:

as DUBLINER: Am I late? Half an hour? God bless us, this is a terrible city for time. Sure the day'd be gone before you have your prayers said. Ah, I was working away like the devil. There's a stream of sweat down me back like the Shannon. I didn't stop or stay for a cup of tea. Just a couple of drinks and away with me. I met Seanin in Mooney's. He won't be here tonight. Between you and me he's up to his eyes in this IRA split. Ah, sure he wouldn't be much good to you if he was here. Footless. Sure I'll do his part. The unfortunate devil is no good in it anyway.

MAC LÍAMMÓIR: But the plays went on. It was the burning, unwavering flame that glows under the mockery, the sodden drunkenness, the rain dark clouds of indifference and folly. This made them happen.

This has always been my fear for the rebirth of Irish Ireland: *And is it worth it?* This search for a flickering light no bigger than a candle flame. One thing is certain. If it is left alone in the wind and rain for a single generation, it will die.

But if it blazes up into what we believe was its former brightness, what then?

And there was fear: that, having at last blown back life into the gentle woman we loved, we might one day be confronted with a Frankenstein's monster.

Meanwhile, I was growing tired.

We had been approached by the British Council at the request of the Egyptian Government to make a tour of Egypt.

Edward, like the Old Lady, said 'No'. The word 'British' was a red rag to the Etonian bull.

We both fought like steers. Here was the opportunity to take Irish theatre abroad. To do what we thought our theatre should do. To show Ireland to the world and, more importantly, to show the world to Ireland. We argued the artistic case with Edward.

And I worried about Hilton. What had I done bringing him to a foreign land with all his English energy and idealism. What was here for him?

as HILTON: I'm not Irish. I haven't a passion to rebuild walls that aren't even mine. Oh yes, I like it here. I want to be with you. Ireland may need you, England doesn't need me. But England means London, and London means a result sooner or later. It means a final answer to one's worth. It has ultimate standards, aims, definitions. It has a policy. In Ireland, you talk all day long and grope about in a fog. You pat each other on the back and tear each other to pieces and none of it means a thing.

The press can't tell the difference between a drama and a pig fair. And a schoolboy's performance of Hamlet in Mullingar is compared with Olivier's.

We've got to expand or go under. We must get out. Oh, not for good. But we must get out and develop or stay here and stagnate. London was too soon. We weren't ready for it.

I wish I could see a new form. A sort of Elizabethanism, a simplicity. You don't know how sick I am of all that paint and canvas. A half-hearted attempt to create an impossible illusion.

I believe in the direct contact. The taking of the audience into one's confidence. A sort of music hall intimacy: 'A funny thing happened on the way to the theatre tonight.'

That's how Shakespeare wrote, I'm certain of it. 'You that look pale and tremble at this act'. That 'you'. That's the audience, you see. 'Had I but time'. See the thrill, see the contact. The audience becoming part of the play. Assisting, the French say. Oh, what's the use! The *Irish Times* would say it was neither convincing nor natural and the *Independent* that it was a pity we were doing foreign plays. Sure, hadn't we enough of our own great writers?

MAC LÍAMMÓIR: The argument with Edward trundled on and on until at last he said:

as **LORD LONGFORD:** Very well, then. But it must be on your own financial responsibility.

MAC LÍAMMÓIR: And we went. It was only when we reached Cairo, and just before the opening night, that we discovered that Edward had decided to experiment with his own company. And was to play again in London. With the Dublin Gate Theatre. Our theatre. Hilton's and mine.

The Egyptian season was a great success and we came back to Dublin with a few pounds in our pockets.

At the end of the day, it was decided that Longford and ourselves would share the theatre, six months each, and that the title was ours. Edwards-mac Líammóir Productions, Dublin Gate Theatre.

As Denis Johnston said: 'Til bankruptcy do you part.'

And we went on. Found new writers, new actors. And Mac came and played Othello at the Gate for us and filled the house night after night.

One day I wandered into the auditorium where Hilton was giving an audition.

It was tall, young and chubby. It was interesting. And had distinctly Chinese eyes, like Mac in *Fu Manchu.* And a sort of tropic grace; the jungle struggling for mastery over the city. He ambled like a tiger in a cage. The voice with its brazen transatlantic sonority of power. He looked at us with a little impatience, as though he were giving us the chance to do something beautiful at last. And if we lost our chance, well, sir, it was just too bad.

He was precisely what he himself would have chosen had God consulted him about his birth.

In fact, he wouldn't have changed a single thing.

And at the end of this disgraceful trumpeting Hilton said:

as HILTON [*to* MAC LÍAMMÓIR]: Well, that was bloody awful, wasn't it? But he can play the part. [*To* WELLES] By the way, what's your name?

as ORSON WELLES: I thought you'd got it. Orson Welles.

MAC LÍAMMÓIR: And Orson came thundering into our lives. Thank God, he has never left them.

But completely wrong for Julius Caesar. And for Brutus, I found a handsome young actor whose icy, English smile froze my heart, but whose acting I admired and envied. And James Mason came into our lives, too.

And we toured Europe again to try to make some money. To lose again in Dublin.

And suddenly I noticed that Hilton had begun to wear spectacles when he read. The elephant was older, if not tamer. But I? Ah, the self. One never notices the self. Other people do that.

In 1938 we were touring Europe.

'We are so happy to see you, but why have you come? Why?' asked a distracted notability. 'You should go back at once to your own country.'

'You see those soldiers who are marching? That is what I mean. Today or tomorrow it will come. And next day we are all dead.'

And for the first time I began to be frightened.

'What? The war, of course. No, please, I beg of you do not speak German in public. The people here think England will join up with Hitler at any moment. If they hear an English actor speaking German, they will be sure of it.'

We were in the Balkans. And I was so astonished by this that I forgot to be offended at being called an *English* actor.

Beware in Bucharest, my son,
Beware the awful Bogomil.

But, closely followed by the Third Reich, we managed to get back to Dublin.

At home, we rehearsed Clemence Dane's *Will Shakespeare*.

One morning Isa Hughes came weeping down the aisle. 'England has declared war on Germany.'

For winds may blow, and barley grow
Without you, without you,
And the world get on without you,
Oh, London Town.

Ireland's neutrality was accepted by all.

Though Hilton said, acidly; 'Oh, yes. Neutral. But on whose side?'

And we held aloof.

After all, we were a nation once again. Or almost. Someone else at the Gate had asked, 'Who are we neutral against?'

The world would get on without us. We would get on without the world. Ourselves Alone.

And what was there for the arts in Ireland? The fact of neutrality and geographical isolation should have given them space to develop.

But I have always thought it is a mistake to think the arts can ever develop in isolation.

They did not develop.

Life is a long rehearsal for a play which is never produced, I said to Hilton. The Gate's a drama with no curtain line.

as HILTON: Really? Well, what do you say to this? It came tonight. *Here's* your curtain line. Oh no, not what we are going do next. It's from the Dublin Corporation. The Gate's been condemned. It's too old. It's not suitable.

Still, I like looking at the future. It's unwritten. You can do what you like with it.

MAC LÍAMMÓIR: *For winds may blow, and barley grow,*
Without you, without you.
And the world get on without you,
Oh, London Town

TANNOY: Stand by, Mr. mac Líammóir, please. We're all waiting on you.

Mac Líammóir rises and disappears behind the screen. In a moment he reappears. Straight backed, poised, elegant. He moves down centre.

MAC LÍAMMÓIR: Will somebody come and help me please? I can't see, do you see. I don't know where the entrance is. [*Pause*]

Please.

He waits and the lights fade to black.

ACT II

January, 1978. The drawing room of 4, Harcourt Terrace. The windows look out over the canal and beyond to the Georgian houses of Aylesbury Road. There is a table. A silver cigarette box and lighter. Crystal ashtray and bottles of medicine. On table beside armchair. MAC LIAMMÓIR *is leaning on stick looking out of downstage window.*

MAC LÍAMMÓIR: Old age. Whenever people tell you that it has its advantages, don't believe them. It's hell. Sheer hell. Maud Gonne first told me that. I was fifty then—admitting to forty-five—but knew that she was right.

My God, she was right. What time is it? Quarter past four and nearly dark, dark. The dim twilight of a bitter January evening.

What a pretty sound. *The Dim Twilight. The Celtic Twilight. Götterdämmerung. Twilight of the Gods.*

How cleverly the Romantics made the disagreeable agreeable. Silly creatures. And for how long I was taken in by them. Shakespeare was so much more sensible. Sympathetic. Empathetic. Crabbed age. No youth together.

Oh, heavens. If you do love old men; if you yourselves be old.

And every fair from fair sometimes declines
By chance, and nature's changing course, untrimmed.
But thy eternal summer shall not fade.

How are ye?

And how dreadful to be the same age as this dreadful century. 'The tragedy of age is not that one is old; but that one is young.'

Time becomes chilly and remote and less and less familiar. And one's own place in it of little consequence.

I am not convinced that Faustus' bargain was such a very bad one. Despite all that blood streaming in the firmament. Of course, Marlowe was always inclined to be unrestrained. To go too far. At least there was Mephistopheles—who seemed quite fun. And Helen of Troy.

We toured Europe after *Othello* had, at last, been made and before it had been released.

A World Tour, Orson had said. And we were at once back with the idea of the Elizabethan theatre.

Hilton was over the moon. To be truthful, so was I.

Importance, of course. Drastically cut. By me. With me as Algy, Orson as John/Ernest swiping Lady Bracknell's best lines and Hilton as Canon Chasuble. *Richard III*, Orson as Richard wearing the largest hump seen outside London Zoo. And cut to half an hour. *Faust*—Goethe not Marlowe with large chunks of Milton and Welles thrown in.

And we had heard, in some Paris nightclub, a young, black chanteuse with all the charm of The Little Match Girl dressed up as The Wicked Stepmother. And Orson said:

as ORSON WELLES: Of course Helen of Troy was black. No, don't, dearest Micheál, please don't ask 'Why?' with that apparently intelligent but, in fact, totally moronic expression on your face. Of course Helen of Troy was black. You'll be asking me next why the horse was wooden, goddammit!

MAC LÍAMMÓIR: So Eartha Kitt was Helen.

And nothing lasted more than twenty minutes. Potted classics from potty actors. Orson and I, two ageing but vivacious juvenile leads.

A World Tour with three actors—Orson, Hilton and Me.

And Eartha.

And *A Saint in Hollywood,* a trifle by Orson himself.

Oh, and Conjuring Tricks from Orson.

These, I need hardly say, were the wild success of the whole tour to Orson's scarcely concealed satisfaction and Hilton's and my fury.

The Third Man was the current film rage and everywhere we went we were greeted by 'The Harry Lime Theme'. Which drove Orson mad. Because he hadn't written it himself. Like the Cuckoo Clock speech.

We were desperate for money. But I don't think Orson made any. And we not much. But, though there was rarely any money in our pockets, we lived in as much luxury as could be found in Europe after the war. Whatever the pundits say, war is not glamorous.

At the very best hotels which had given themselves a lick of paint and a facelift and tried to disguise food shortages with very large orchestras. Which played *The Blue Danube* incessantly.

Except when we appeared, when they played 'The Harry Lime Theme'.

And all this after a year of shooting *Othello* for which we had hoped for large sums of money.

But Orson *had* no money so we got the World Tour instead.

Once, during *Othello,* I went back to Dublin while Orson was reshooting scenes for which I was not needed.

The Gate was playing in Cork and then Belfast.

I went to see Maud Gonne to tell her about *Othello* and to say

'Goodbye'. For I knew she would not be with us much longer. She talked warmly, as usual. About life, about art.

She liked poor people and birds and her son, Sean. And she talked of Ireland and how she hoped that Hilton and I would learn to make films for it.

She was the ruin of a gaunt, cavernous beauty. The woman who had inspired some of the best love poems ever written.

Of course, you couldn't be with her for five minutes without being reminded of them.

Age had brought an increasing gentleness and humour.

Though she will remain forever a partisan, the splendour of her years passed alternately in revolutionary conspiracy and in long terms of imprisonment, that portion of her mind which Yeats described as 'all but turned to stone', is, somehow, perceived by herself, and as delicately passed by, as one passes in time of peace by a monument to the tragedies of war.

As she talked, I looked at her and thought: there she is— 'The Phoenix' who 'lived in storm and strife.'

But then I thought that Yeats had got it wrong.

Your small hands are not beautiful,
And I am afraid that you will run
And paddle to the wrist
In that mysterious, always brimming lake
Where those that have obeyed the holy law
Paddle and are perfect; leave unchanged
The hands that I have kissed
For old sake's time.

Well, to me, her hands were beautiful.

Then a quick trip to Belfast to catch the last night of *Where*

Stars Walk, at the Grand Opera House, before flying back to Rome.

Impossible to fathom why I like that strange, northern city. But I do. Admittedly, a cold, ugly sort of place, even in radiant April sunshine.

Blotched with *fin de siècle* mansions and fussy streets full of cake shops.

But there's something about it all. Its frantic practicability? Its bleak bowler hatted refusal of the inevitable? What is it?

We had first played in Belfast at the beginning of the war. And to our surprise Mac had said:

as MCMASTER: Belfast is dead, dear, dead. And you can't get a drink for love or money on a Sunday. And they only like the pictures.

You must remember that my Aunt Mary, that's the red nosed one, Hilton, married an Orangeman. Such a disgrace, dear.

MAC LÍAMMÓIR: We were a success

There was of course, the question of the National Anthem. And two staunchly republican members of the company who refused to stand for it.

And neither Hilton's firm, no-nonsense approach or my self-conscious blarneying could shift them.

But the rest of us rather enjoyed it. And sang 'God Save the King' with zest every night.

And the audiences appreciated it.

No, there was no trouble in Belfast. Except ... Well, there was *The Old Lady Says 'No'!*

The Opera House Board was not too keen.

as BELFASTMAN: *The Old Lady Says 'No'!?* A play about Robert Emmet? Now just you listen to me. I wouldn't go to see a play about Robert Emmet if you give me five hundred pounds here in my hand. And I'm broad-minded, mind you!

MAC LÍAMMÓIR: Hilton played the English ruler to the manner born. Well, he was to the manner born, of course. And gave a brisk lecture on Denis Johnston's British credentials. Not many.

We played *The Old Lady* and filled the house. Belfast adored it and the curtain calls, minus the republicans, were endless.

And then, on the 17th April, the Irish Republic was declared. Felt very *emotional* and sent off telegrams to Dev and Maud Gonne and others.

Hilton and I drank to the new State and H. piously thanked God that England was at last free of 700 years of Irish domination.

We stayed at the Crawfordsburn Inn.

Hilton retired to bed and I was inspired to drink the Republic's health with a compatriot. So rang the bell and summoned the liftman.

On his appearance says I: 'Would you like to drink to the Republic?'

Liftman's face, a vivid and trying shade of blue, brightened at the word 'drink', but developed hitherto unnoticed network of veins at the mention of 'Republic' and asked, with great suspicion, 'What Republic?' And, on being enlightened, stated firmly that he was a devout Unionist.

So there.

Plus ça change, plus c'est la même chose.

And I wondered, not for the first time, what would happen to the arts in Ireland now that we were so gloriously free.

Free to do what?

What, in God's name, was she to do now that she was no longer the Princess in the Tower, superbly menaced by the Dragon posing as St. George?

The border question, of course, is pressing but hardly possesses the statue of a Villain and art, like religion and life, must have its Villain.

I knew that there would be a slump in Irish letters. We can't really go on about 1916, or 1922 or even 1969 for very much longer.

I can only think about the 1950s as maddening.

After the World Tour we returned to Dublin practically destitute.

On the covers of *Picturegoer* and *Pictureshow*, Orson's and my face beamed triumphantly. But people didn't know that we had no money. None. The six thousand pounds which I was to be paid for Iago wasn't there. And there was nothing to be done about it. For Orson hadn't got it either.

Terence de Vere White, a Dublin solicitor with a literary bent, was trying to sort out our affairs. And the bills kept coming in.

The telephone was cut off. And we had to have a pay as you speak one put in. Which meant having great piles of pennies ready.

And one day Terence rang to say that he had heard from a Sheriff of the Court, who, he said, was embarrassed and sympathetic, that the Bailiffs Were Coming. It was a depressing time. We sent the staff (all unpaid for weeks) away for two days and Hilton and I waited, like Oscar at the Cadogan Hotel, for the Dreaded Knock.

It came at three o clock.

Hilton immediately made off through the back garden

carrying a suitcase full of all the silver we had, as well as two pictures by Jack Yeats.

I, carefully dressed in a Japanese kimono and wearing a little more make up than usual—nice slinky, heavily mascaraed eyes—descended the stairs and, looking like an overweight Madame Butterfly, opened the front door.

I Smiled a Welcome. I pouted rouged lips; I lowered my eyelashes. And raised them again, invitingly. Elizabeth Arden had never worked so hard.

The Bailiffs fled.

Most exhausting. And a performance that was well worth 7/6 at the box office.

The Gate needed a good many more 7/6 to keep open.

But there were good moments. Hilton played Mr. Micawber in a BBC television serial. And I played Oscar Wilde in a television reconstruction of the trial which was well received. And I adapted *The Informer* for the stage. And, against all advice, including Hilton's I played Gyppo Nolan.

And won them all over, despite their uncalled for reservations.

Then out of the blue came Maura Laverty, who wrote *Tolka Row* for us. Which ran and ran and toured and toured. For years and years.

But the years were grinding, and Hilton and I were growing old. And perhaps stamina was wilting.

Then in 1954, I toured Europe and played in London in *Hedda Gabler*, with Peggy Ashcroft and Rachael Kempson. It was directed by Peter Ashford and one day we had lunch together in Amsterdam. We were in a lazy, silly mood and lingered over coffee and liqueurs. And Peter said:

as PETER ASHFORD: 'The studio was filled with the rich odour of roses.'

MAC LÍAMMÓIR: And I said: 'And from the corner of the divan of Persian saddle bags where he was lying, smoking, as was his custom, innumerable cigarettes, Lord Henry Wotton, could just catch the gleam of the honey sweet and honey coloured blossoms of a laburnum, whose tremulous branches seemed hardly able to bear the burden of a beauty so flamelike as theirs.'

Peter bounced up and down in his chair and, in an excess of delirium, ordered two more yellow Chartreuses.

We went on getting sillier and sillier. And sounding more and more like Robert Hichens' *The Green Carnation* and less and less like Oscar.

The yellow Chartreuse arrived and it wasn't yellow at all but a rather depressing, greeny mustard.

Peter said: 'You must do it you know, Micheál.' And we parted with the great stateliness of the semi-intoxicated.

And that was all and Oscar disappeared into the shadows.

Hedda Gabler kept us going for a while. But Gate Theatre Productions seemed to be dead. With the pay now demanded by the most inexperienced actors, it was no longer feasible to do big cast plays.

But big cast plays were Hilton's speciality. Lennox Robinson once said: 'You are quite wonderful, Hilton, the way you make twenty people look like twenty-two.'

Then we found Brian Friel for the Gate. And the best play about Ireland that I had read since *The Old Lady*. *Philadelphia Here I Come* was a huge success and we could use the telephone again without resorting to a sordid little pile of coins.

It went to Broadway and was a big success there too.

All very well for Paddy Bedford but what about me? No parts for me.

It was strange to see Paddy, as dark and shining as a diamond, play the leads in my old plays, written for me.

Hilton and I were both forced to take separate engagements, whenever they were offered. Which wasn't as often as you might think.

Yet we were apart for much of the time.

And when not apart we quarrelled. Ferociously. I thought of Swift. Often. And the poisoned rat in a trap. The trap that I had made for myself. And Hilton. And, short of chewing our legs off, there seemed to be no way out of this backwater in our careers.

Now the question was: what would we do for the Dublin festival? We had nothing. And it would be the first time that the Gate had made no contribution.

It was Patrick McLarnon who first suggested a one-man show.

as PATRICK MCLARNON: You should do a show on Wilde? Now, why not? You're the only one who could do it. Look at Gielgud. He's doing Shakespeare. *Seven Ages of Man.*

MAC LÍAMMÓIR: But he's Gielgud. And he has Shakespeare on his side. At least I *think* he has.

as PATRICK MCLARNON: Well, you've got Oscar. Now come on, Micheál. Do it. Now, lets tell Hilton and save him going through all those dreary scripts.

MAC LÍAMMÓIR: I thought, well, maybe. And I called up to Hilton.

Hilton! Patrick has had a wonderful idea for a show about Oscar Wilde.

And he called down:

as HILTON: Then fucking well get on with it.

MAC LÍAMMÓIR: I love encouragement.

And I got on with it.

In fact, I got on with it all through *Where the Rainbow Ends.* Which was one of the shows I did to keep us afloat.

And Hilton was, for, the moment, happy that he could leave Drama at RTE. For, though the three thousand a year had saved us from the poorhouse, it was distinctly unsatisfying to him artistically.

And, perhaps too many of my own plays had been put on air. But the medium kills writers. And, in those days, not enough writers had learned to use the medium; if, indeed, they have today.

I heard a little rhyme which amused me and infuriated Hilton. But which summarised his difficulties.

There was an old man of Montrose
With small eyes and a very big nose.
Who did plays by the score
By mac Líammóir
That wily old man of Montrose.

Another difficulty was that new writing had been associated with the Gate. So it was natural that Hilton should look to our own writers for material.

And during *Where the Rainbow Ends* I worked on *Oscar.*

A young Irish actor, whom I had known when he was with Mac, and who was in the show, offered to dress me.

Much more to the point, he offered to type out my notes and do a little research.

And *Oscar* got on like a house on fire.

And back in Dublin we got ready to present it. So far, without a title. We thought of them all. *Rise and Fall of an Aesthete, The Green Carnation, The Happy Prince, From Merrion Square to Reading Gaol,* which sounded to me like a G.W. Henty Adventure Story for Boys—*From Powder Monkey to Admiral.*

They were all dismissed. And then one morning as I lay supine in the bath, with Hilton in pyjama trousers, whirling in and out and brandishing a shaving brush, still, even at that hour in the morning, hot on the trail of a myriad new suggestions, I rebelled and shouted: 'Is a title of such supreme importance?'

as HILTON: Wilde thought so. He had 'Importance' on the brain. *Woman of No Importance, Importance of Being Ernest.*

MAC LÍAMMÓIR: Well, call it *Importance of Being Wilde,* for God's sake!

as HILTON: Oh God, you Irish. No stamina. None at all. But that's not bad. Not bad. *The Importance of Being Wilde.* But the rhythm's wrong. It must be the same. One syllable's no good. It should have two. It *must* have two.

That's my talc you're using. Not that I mind. God knows you're welcome to anything I have. But you won't put it back. I know you. Age cannot wither nor custom stale your infinite kleptomania. You're hell to work with. Always have been. No concentration. Never did have. And don't start glaring at me. Your Lorca Fandangos have no effect on me at all. None whatever. *Two* syllables. It's essential.

What am I talking about? Oh, God preserve me from Irish people. Ernest, of course. That's it. I've got it. I've got it! *Importance of Being Oscar.*

MAC LÍAMMÓIR: The *Importance of Being Oscar,* I corrected him.

It was the only way to preserve any dignity at all.

But the coffee that morning tasted good. And we drank it together.

In 1960, just before *Oscar,* I quarrelled with Orson. It was a foolish one and, though we have since kissed and made up, things have not been quite the same.

I was alone in the house late one night when the telephone rang. It was Orson. He was filming the Falstaff/Prince Hal relationship. Calling it *Chimes at Midnight.*

Naturally I was excited. We had often discussed the 'Histories' together and thought that with Hal and Falstaff an interesting and novel theme of historical significance would emerge.

He offered me the part of Henry IV. I was aghast. Naturally, I had supposed that I would play Prince Hal.

You see, Hilton was away. I can't think where. I had no advice. Terence de Vere White rushed round to soothe me. And I was told, to my great annoyance, what a good part Henry was.

I was foolish. I was silly. That's what is so unforgivable. John Gielgud played the part. He was wonderful.

Ah well.

But the tour of *Oscar* was a great consolation. Which I played in every capital in the world. And, for the first time we didn't have to worry about money.

Or even the state of the Gate.

And then in 1962. After a long separation I would be working again with the great Mac. He Othello, me Iago.

The realisation of many a dream. But it was not to be. Just as Death had snatched Máire from me in Monte Carlo, he lay in wait for Mac in the shelly banks of Sandymount and before rehearsals even began Mac was mortally struck. He was never ill. Every day of his life he swam in Dublin Bay. With Anna Pavlova, his Russian Samoyed dog.

Hoping against hope, I went to see him.

as MCMASTER: Well that's that, dear. The doctors looked askance, as you might say, at me X-rays. I have to rest, dear—me rest! Maybe next festival. No, Micky—the curtain won't go up on that one.

MAC LÍAMMÓIR: And that night, when Marjorie went to make their last cup of tea, the telephone rang. It was Dot, my sister in England. And Marjorie said that Mac was well and only needed rest.

When she went back to the drawing room, he was dead. Still looking out over the sea.

But I *knew*—there was nothing else for him to do, you see. Mary Rose agrees. He couldn't act; so he just died. It was cruel of him. It was selfish. The Greek God was dead. What about Ganymede? What about me? Later in Egypt, I tried to tell a group of journalists about the Irish theatre.

Someone asked: 'And Anew McMaster?'

[*As if to interviewer*] Know him? A romantic comet. A wastrel. The gods were too good to him. He had the body, the face and the voice which make other people writhe with envy. A boundless sense of poetry and the brain of a man half eagle half child.

Normal life means nothing to him. He can only function on the stage in the presence of love and birth, war and death.

His speaking of such lines as: 'Whose eyes dropped tears as fast as the Arabian/Trees their medicinable gums' ring in the ears for days afterwards.

It was for lips like his that great speeches were written.

And I would rather spend an hour in his company than a lifetime with any other Irish actor I know.

[*Returning to normal*] As with Máire, I never dreamed of him. As with Máire, he is with me always.

I was made a Doctor of Literature at Dublin University. And when the telephone rang and Hilton was asked for Dr. mac Líammóir, he would say:

as HILTON: Dr. mac Líammóir is operating abroad, this is Nurse Edwards speaking.

MAC LÍAMMÓIR: Which I thought was funny. But we were apart a lot of the time.

I can say that the idea of doing a one-man show had never entered my mind. Since they had always seemed to me the prerogative of the female sex.

One of whose most breathtaking members, Ruth Draper, was still doing it. And whom I genuinely believed to be a supreme artist.

But the pretty, essential props, hats, shawls a handbag or two were not useful to the male. What could one do with a bowler hat and a couple of trick moustaches?

For a visual magic seemed to me to be the essential ingredient for success.

I wondered vaguely why I was so pleased when my fellow actors disappeared offstage and left me to get on with: *O, what a rogue and peasant slave am I.*

Or why there was such lurid satisfaction in the line: *Ay so:—God be with ye.*
Now I am alone.

The freedom was enchanting. So was the certainty that nothing could break in upon one's dream short of the theatre collapsing around one's head. One was alone with the audience and with God or the Devil, whichever happened to be in one's heart.

But these were only moments. Sooner or later they would

come back, those fellow shadows with whom one worked. Teamwork: comradeship, brotherly labour, the simultaneous dedication to a mutually practised art.

In a one-man show, one was, indeed, alone.

And on tour, lonely.

Hilton threatened to advertise for a partner 'Incapable of doing a one-man show.'

He had directed Donald Wolfit in *Tambourlane* at the Old Vic. It had been a huge success and acclaimed by Tynan. But nothing happened.

In the dramatic arts, the past is not only another country, but its citizens *persona non grata.*

And I wonder with what uncertainty, with what nervousness the present demands the dismissal of all that has gone before.

How can you plan the future but by reference to the past? Past, present and future are not different territories. In conflict for the glittering prize. They are the same. Seen from a different perspective.

A new aggression pervades all of life.

And the Graces are fled. From life, too, it seems.

As when a well-graced actor leaves the stage.

Discretion has come to mean pusillanimity and low spiritedness.

A delegation of 'gays' came to see me in Dublin after *Oscar*. Would I declare in the press that I was homosexual? Would I lead a 'Gay Rights' parade?

Maddened by that most inappropriate of words, I was churlish. Their enthusiasm was endearing, their naivety irritating.

I said 'no'; why couldn't they just be queer, like the rest of us?

But it is a worry. Though no longer for me.

And was it cowardice to withdraw from a battle in which I had never thought it necessary to fight?

Neither Noël nor I have ever wanted a contest on those grounds. We have yielded to the times and eagerly, gaily, you might say, subverted them.

Like Oscar, though more successfully.

Neither Noël nor I would have waited in the Cadogan Hotel. Or in my case, the Shelbourne.

It was in the brilliant, riotous blue and gold of South Africa that I began to go blind.

And I felt the chill of the dark night.

It was a dimness, a peripherary shadow, and for as long as I could, I ignored it. It didn't go away. I thought, think to this day, that it was the result of Klieg Lights in *Othello*. Though no-one agreed with me.

Not to be able to see the vividness of colour. The look of black words on white paper creating a golden world. Now I was read to. I hated it. A reader is an editor. Coming between me and the work. However good the reader.

I tried to be grateful. Without being hateful.

And Mary Rose McMaster helped me to learn lines. For I still did the occasional new play.

Tony Guthrie directed one. It was not a success. I played Swift. Couldn't learn it. A nightmare.

Poor Tony. Losing my temper, I told him that his jam was no good either.

Which was true.

I last played *Oscar* at the Gate in Easter Week, 1975. Just before we opened I had what the doctors described as an aneurism, a stroke. Which restricted my movement. So I played most of it on the chaise longue. And added cigarettes to give an illusion of activity.

On the last night the President, Erskine Childers, made an embarrassing speech.

It was done.

And the government suddenly found some money, and after nearly fifty years, the Gate was secure.

Too late. Far, far too late.

All your life you fight for the crown, and when you get it you no longer have the energy to wear it.

I tried to supervise the costumes in new productions.

Time passed slowly.

Dear Patricia Turner came to work with us. And made me laugh. And looked after my clothes. Just as well, for once, getting ready for a reception at Aras an Uachtarain, I couldn't fasten my trousers. Patricia explained that they were on backwards.

I had more time to think. But about what?

Friends here, and in England, continued to die.

I remember Noël saying to Hilton and me that all he asked now was that his friends didn't die during lunch.

My old friend, Desmond Rushe of the *Independent* came to see me the other day and, as we were talking, he said:

as DESMOND RUSHE: Do you believe in God?

MAC LÍAMMÓIR: And I said, Yes. Certainly. Oh, I don't believe in the teaching of the churches whose job it is to maintain the powers that be.

And I certainly don't believe in Hell. I used to think that Life was like a rehearsal. If we don't get it right, then we come back again next day and try again. Until we do get it right.

He asked me what made me happy . I could think of nothing. Except Hilton being well, and happy.

He isn't well.

And we talked of whom we would like to meet from the past.

Once when I was being interviewed on television, I mentioned that I had seen Nijinsky, not once but many times.

And the interviewer had stopped—it was in Europe, of course, not in these sceptical northern islands—and said:

as INTERVIEWER: Let me look into your eyes. C'est incroyable! These eyes have seen Him.

MAC LÍAMMÓIR: And I thought, how wonderful to have done something so perfect that, long years after, a young man who had never seen him should remember and want to look into the eyes that had seen the miracle that was Nijinsky.

How wonderful at the end of life to have done one perfect thing. Written one perfect sonnet. Composed a single sonata. Given one perfect performance.

It is what all artists want. Pray for.

Not all television interviewers are so thoughtful; so reflective. Once in Ireland I was speaking of language; of nationality. Of how words tell us who we are. And I had just said that the English equivalent of mac Líammóir was Willmore. That in my childhood in England I had acted under the name of Michael Willmore.

as INTERVIEWER: So, does that mean that you aren't as Irish as all that?

MAC LÍAMMÓIR: As all what? I speak and write in Irish. I have loved the country since nationality meant anything to me at all. I have worked with my partner to build up its theatre and its drama. To show its virtues to the world. And, when I travel, I do so on a passport signed personally by the country's founder, Eamon de Valéra.

As Irish as all what?

And what does it mean to say that one loves one's country?

Desmond and I continued our talk as to whom we should like to meet in the next world. Curiously, I didn't say Shakespeare for I have known him all my life. But I thought, Chopin. Listening to him, I get the oddest feeling that I understand him.

And now, of course, we no longer have a curtain to bring down. So the play is never really over. It just makes way for new characters. New players, new plots.

And Hilton and I? And Orson? And Mac. And Marjorie, now lying in a tiny coffin beside him at last.

At the Gate, it will soon be time to go onstage.

And the call boy will knock on the dressing room door.

Half an hour, please. Half an hour.

And later:

Stand by. The Curtain's just gone up, sir.

> *Lights begin to fade, slowly. Fade to Black.*